REASONS WHY PLASTIC SHOULD BE BANNED WITH RECYCLE

AN ESSAY ON PLASTICS ADVANTAGE & DISADVANTAGES & ALTERNATIVE

SANDEEP RAVIDAS

Contents

CHAPTER ONE

Introduction

An Introduction

Plastics are a wide range of synthetic or semi-synthetic materials that use polymers as a main ingredient. Their plasticity makes it possible for plastics to be moulded, extruded or pressed into solid objects of various shapes. This adaptability, plus a wide range of other properties, such as being lightweight, durable, flexible, and inexpensive to produce, has led to its widespread use. Plastics typically are made through human industrial systems. Most modern plastics are derived from fossil fuel-based chemicals like natural gas or petroleum; however, recent industrial methods use variants made from renewable materials, such as corn or cotton derivatives.

9.2 billion tonnes of plastic are estimated to have been made between 1950 and 2017. More than half this plastic has been produced since 2004. In 2020, 400 million tonnes of plastic were produced. If global trends on plastic demand continue, it is estimated that by 2050 annual global plastic production will reach over 1,100 million tonnes.

In developed economies, about a third of plastic is used in packaging and roughly the same in buildings in applications such as piping, plumbing or vinyl siding. Other uses include automobiles (up to 20% plastic), furniture, and toys. In the developing world, the applications of plastic may differ; 42% of India's consumption is used in packaging. In the medical field, polymer implants and other medical devices are derived at least partially from plastic. Worldwide, about 50 kg of plastic is produced annually per person, with production doubling every ten years.

The success and dominance of plastics starting in the early 20th century has caused widespread environmental problems, due to their slow decomposition rate in natural ecosystems. Toward the end of the 20th century, the plastics industry promoted recycling in order to ease environmental concerns while continuing to produce virgin plastic and to push the responsibility of plastic pollution onto the consumer. The main companies producing plastics doubted the economic viability of recycling at the time, and the economic viability has never improved. Plastic collection and recycling is largely ineffective because of failures of contemporary complexity required in cleaning and sorting post-consumer plastics for effective reuse. Most plastic produced has not been reused, either being captured in landfills or persisting in the environment as plastic pollution. Plastic pollution can be found in all the world's major water bodies, for example, creating garbage patches in all of the world's oceans and contaminating terrestrial ecosystems. Of all the plastic discarded so far, some 14% has been incinerated and less than 10% has been recycled.

We can recycle plastic, and everyone should try to use recycled products instead of throwing them into landfills. The best way to reduce plastic wastage is through the 3 R's – reduce, reuse and recycle. Plastic can also be toxic when burned and results in plastic pollution. The environmental impact of plastic is vast because plastic takes up space in landfills, where it contaminates the land most of the time. Finding a way to reuse and recycle plastic would reduce these problems while keeping our environment safe. Teach kids the harm that plastic can do to our precious planet by referring to an essay on should plastic be banned.

CHAPTER TWO

Brief On Plastics

Before knowing reasons we should know what is plastics. So, Plastics are a wide range of semi-synthetic or synthetic substances that contains polymers as their main ingredient. The plasticity during production enables the plastic to be moulded, extruded or pressed into solid objects of different shapes. It makes the material to be able to adapt accordingly and is useful in various ranges of applications.

This adaptability, plus a wide variety of beneficial properties, such as being lightweight, durable and flexible, alongside cheap manufacturing methods, has contributed to widespread acceptance in contemporary society. Most modern plastics come from fossil fuel-based petrochemicals such as natural gas or petroleum. However, the most recent plastic manufacturing processes use alternatives manufactured from renewable materials such as corn or cotton derivatives.

The word plastic comes from the Greek word "plastikos" meaning "capable of being shaped or moulded" and, in turn, from "plastos" meaning "moulded".

The plasticity or the state of the malleability of material during the manufacturing process enables it to be cast, pressed or extruded into various shapes, such as films, fibre, plate, tube, bottles, boxes, among many other such examples. The usual noun plastic form should not be confused with the technical adjective plastic form. The adjective shall refer to any material which undergoes a plastic deformation or a permanent change of shape when strained beyond a particular limit. For example, the stamped or forged aluminium exhibits plasticity in this context, but is not plastic in common sense. On the other hand, certain plastics, in their finished form, can break before deformation and are thus technically not plastic.

CHAPTER THREE

Plastics: Properties and Classifications:

Properties and Classifications:

Plastics generally categorize as the chemical structure of the polymer base and side chains. The major categories of these classifications include acrylics, polyesters, silicones, polyurethanes and halogenated plastics. Plastics also categorize by the chemical process used in their syntheses, such as cross-linking, condensation, and polyaddition.

Plastics can also categorize by their various physical properties, such as tensile strength, hardness, resistance to heat, density, and glass transition temperature, and their chemical properties, such as organic polymer chemistry and its resistance and its reactions to various other chemical materials and processes, such as ionizing radiation, oxidation and organic solvents. Other classifications depend on characteristics that are relevant to the manufacturing process or designing of the product. Examples of such qualities and classes are conductive polymers, thermoplastics and thermosets, engineering plastics and biodegradable plastics and other similar plastics with unique structures, such as elastomers.

- Thermoplastics: Thermoplastics are plastics that do not undergo a chemical change in their composition when heated, and hence, they can mould several times. Examples are polypropylene (PP), polyethylene (PE), polyvinyl chloride (PVC) and polystyrene (PS).
- Thermosets: Thermosets polymers are plastics that can melt and mould into any shape only once. They'll undergo an irreversible chemical reaction when heated, hence, if heated again they decompose instead of melting.
- Conductive Polymers: Intrinsically Conducting Polymers (ICP) are electrically conductive organic polymers. Example: Polyacetylene.
- Biodegradable Plastics: Biodegradable plastics are plastics that degrade or break down when exposed to sunlight or ultraviolet radiation, bacteria, certain enzymes, dampness or water, or wind abrasion. In certain circumstances, rodents, pests or insect attacks can also act ad biodegradation modes or environmental degradation. Example: Starch-based plastics, Cellulose-based plastics, Soy-based plastics.
- Bioplastics: While most plastics are products of petrochemicals, bioplastics are plastics produced substantially from renewable plant materials such as cellulose and starch. Due to the finite limits of petrochemical resources and the risk of global warming, bioplastics is still a growing field.

CHAPTER FOUR

Examples of Plastics

Naturally occurring polymers include tar, shellac, tortoiseshell, animal horn, cellulose, amber, and latex from tree sap. Synthetic polymers include polyethylene (used in plastic bags); polystyrene (used to make Styrofoam cups); polypropylene (used for fibers and bottles); polyvinyl chloride (used for food wrap, bottles, and drain pipe); and polytetrafluoroethylene, or Teflon (used for nonstick surfaces). Although many polymers are hydrocarbons that contain only carbon and hydrogen, other polymers may also contain oxygen, chlorine, fluorine, nitrogen, silicon, phosphorus, and sulfur.

Natural polymers, such as cellulose and latex, were first chemically modified in the 19th century to form celluloid and vulcanized rubber. The first totally synthetic polymer, Bakelite, was produced in 1907. The first semisynthetic fiber, rayon, was developed from cellulose in 1911. However, it was not until the global disruption caused by World War II, when natural sources of latex, wool, silk, and other materials became difficult to obtain, that synthetics were mass produced. Synthetic rubber was needed for tires, and nylon was needed as a replacement for silk for parachutes. Today synthetic polymers in the form of plastics are in wide use, and the plastics industry is one of the fastest growing in the United States and around the world. The industry produces approximately 150 kilograms of polymers per person annually in the United States.

Characteristics of Polymers

Polymers seem to have a limitless range of characteristics along with properties that allow them to be dyed in an endless array of colors. Their properties can be enhanced by additives. Being able to design or engineer polymers for specific applications makes plastics unique materials. Although each polymer has unique characteristics, most polymers have some general properties:

- They are resistant to chemicals.
- They are insulators of heat and electricity.
- They are light in mass and have varying degrees of strength.
- They can be processed in various ways to produce fibers, sheets, foams, or intricate molded parts.

The raw material for manufacturing plastic products is called a resin. Some of the most common resins are polyethylene (PE), polyethylene terephthalate (PET), polypropylene (PP), polyvinyl chloride (PVC), and polystyrene (PS). These resins are often used in packaging. The Recycling Code chart in the linked PDF shows the recycling code for these resins.

CHAPTER SIX

Disadvantage of Plastic

Humans are facing a crisis with plastic bags. They are one of the greatest risks to the environment despite their practicality and versatility. Governments like China have banned plastics, and others have made it illegal to use certain types of bags. Despite the many applications, there's no shortage of reasons why plastic bags should be banned.

- Plastic bags pollute land and water
- Plastic bags are lightweight. They travel far and wide by wind and water. They are not easy to decompose, which means they are left lying all around and floating on oceans and lakes.
- They are made from non-renewable sources
- The raw materials used to make plastic are extracted from natural gas and petroleum. These are non-renewable sources, and their extraction and production emit greenhouse gases that contribute to global change.
- They require a lot of energy to produce
- The energy required to produce nine plastic bags is enough to drive a car for one kilometre. Considering they have a short useful life, it's unfortunate that so much energy is used in making them.
- Plastic bags are toxic
- Plastic bags contain a variety of toxic and harmful chemicals that not only affect the environment but can also affect how our bodies function.
- They don't degrade
- Plastic bags don't decompose. The best they do is get broken down into small pieces that are often airborne and land in oceans.
- Plastic bags are dangerous to wild and marine life
- Once they land in oceans and forests, plastic bags are eaten by animals, causing various health issues, which often result in death.
- Plastic bags are harmful to human health
- Plastic bags contain chemicals that can lead to severe health conditions like cancer when ingested.
- Plastic bags are not easy to recycle
- The recycling rate for plastic bags is about 5%, which is extremely low. What's more, plastic bags can't be reduced to their organic state. Once created, they remain in their synthetic state throughout.
- Plastic bags are produced in massive quantities
- Plastic bag production is too high because they are in high demand, most of which end up in landfills, oceans, and waterways.
- Consumers are reluctant about recycling plastic bags
- Most consumers will toss their plastic bags in the trash or leave them to be blown by the wind. Banning them makes them easier to manage.
- Plastic bags are disposable
- We can all do without plastic bags. There are other options.

- Plastic bags clog storm drains
- Plastic bags find their way to the drainage and sewer system and eventually block them.
- Plastic bags are a major contributor to landfills
- A plastic bag ban would be a big relief on the pressure landfills are experiencing at the moment.
- Bans can reduce plastic bag waste
- A ban would not only reduce plastic bag waste but plastic waste in general.
- A ban can help keep the environment clean
- Most of the trash on the streets comprises of plastic bags. Banning them would keep the streets and the environment cleaner.
- It can save money
- Producing plastic bags is very expensive. There are other more affordable options on the market. Banning plastic could help to save money.
- It is a proven approach in some countries
- Some countries have banned plastic bags with plenty of success, opening up the option to other countries.
- A ban will raise awareness
- A plastic bans would shine the light on the effects of plastic bags creating awareness on their negative impact on the environment.
- The ban would be easy to apply
- Because there are other alternatives to plastic bags like cotton and jute bags, making a transition would be easy.
- It would be a big relief to the governments
- Many governments are currently trying to solve environmental challenges. Banning plastic bags would mean they have one less pollutant to deal with.

There you have it. 20 reasons why plastic bags should be banned for the better of the environment and the economy.

CHAPTER SEVEN

Advantages of Using Plastic

With the growing population and the rising demand for consumer goods, food and beverage manufacturers are constantly looking for ways to enhance their practices and create additional value. They are also required to ensure that the food product is well-preserved using appropriate packaging till the point of sale. While there are multiple alternatives and materials that can be used to package food, plastic food packaging has always been the most preferred option. Plastic has retained this popularity over the years due to its adaptability and durability. Take a look at some of the other benefits plastic food packaging offer:

- Plastic packaging is a very flexible and adaptable form of packaging, which allows manufacturers to customize its shape, size and style as per their customers' requirements.
- Plastic packaging is an extremely light-weight storage option that doesn't require a lot of storage space either. Since they don't take up much storage space, they are also extremely easy to transport, thus reducing the carbon footprint during transportation.
- Plastic packaging can survive extreme environments and don't easily degrade in hot and cold temperatures, thus preserving the integrity of the food or beverage inside it. It also protects your products from moisture, oxygen, dust, light and odours.
- Since plastic is extremely durable and resistant to external influences, you can ensure your product is well-preserved at all times. This in turn, helps you avoid losses due to wastage of inventory and also helps you bring about consistency in product delivery, thus increasing brand value.
- The high versatility of plastic allows for ease of reuse and recycling. In fact, these days' companies are creating specialized plastic bag making machines that help you optimize on the recyclability of plastic.
- The durability offered by plastic packaging also allows manufacturers to print eye-catching, high-quality custom designs, and thereby increase product visibility in a retail setting.
- Plastic packaging is highly economical and can be used by all industries irrespective of their scale of operations. The cost-effectiveness of plastic food packaging is especially beneficial to small-scale product manufacturers as it allows access to standardised packaging options in spite of lower budgets.
- As mentioned above, plastic bags are easily recyclable and require lesser energy to produce in comparison to the other packaging alternatives available. According to a study conducted by United States EPA, plastic bags use 40% less energy to produce and generate 80% less solid waste than paper. The study also revealed a pound of plastic takes 91% less energy to recycle as compared to a pound of paper.

CHAPTER EIGHT

Plastic Recycling

Recently, almost all recycling is performed by simply remelting and reforming used plastic into new items. Additives present risks in recycled products, as they are difficult to remove. When plastic products are recycled, it is highly likely that the additives will be integrated into the new products. Waste plastic, even if it is all of the same polymer type, will contain varying types and amounts of additives. Mixing these together can give a material with inconsistent properties, which can be unappealing to industry. For example, mixing different coloured plastics with different plastic colorants together can produce a discoloured or brown material and for this reason plastic is usually sorted by both polymer type and color before recycling. As additives change the properties of plastics they have to be considered during recycling.

There has been a lot of progress in the plastic ban, especially by the Government. The Government has noticed Plastic Waste Management Amendment Rules, 2021, prohibiting identified single-use plastic items by July 2022. Social media sites only develop methods to reduce the use of single-use plastics, but they also provide information on other ways to reduce them. They have also been a great source of support for people working to create chaos. In addition, plastic awareness is a must for everyone, and it is suggested to read BYJU'S ban on plastic essay.

Many countries have implemented plastic bans. The United Kingdom, France, and China have had bans. Canada is also considering banning the use of plastic bags and straws. To prevent waste created by the pollution caused by plastic, many brands have created new fabrics that can be used instead of plastic. The plastic ban on disposable water bottles is an excellent idea because it will reduce waste and help the environment. However, the Government needs to ensure that all pre-existing containers are recycled instead of thrown away. This will ensure that there is no unnecessary waste and pollution.

CHAPTER NINE

Recycling Codes for Plastic Resins

Recycling Codes for Plastic Resins

Recycling code	Polymer and structure	Uses
1 PETE	$-O-CH_2-CH_2-O-C(=O)-\text{(benzene ring)}-C(=O)-$ Poly(ethylene terephthlate) (PET)	Bottles for soft drinks and other beverages
2 HDPE	$-CH_2-CH_2-CH_2-CH_2-$ High-density polyethylene	Containers for milk and other beverages, squeeze bottles
3 V	$-CH_2-CH(Cl)-CH_2-CH(Cl)-$ Vinyl/polyvinyl chloride	Bottles for cleaning materials, some shampoo bottles
4 LDPE	$-CH_2-CH_2-CH_2-CH_2-$ Low-density polyethylene May have some branches	Plastic bags, some plastic wraps
5 PP	$-CH_2-CH(CH_3)-CH_2-CH(CH_3)-$ Polypropylene	Heavy-duty microwavable containers
6 PS	$-CH_2-CH(\text{phenyl})-CH_2-CH(\text{phenyl})-$ Polystyrene	Beverage/foam cups, toys, window in envelopes
7 Other	All other resins, layered multimaterials, some containers	Some ketchup bottles, snack packs, mixture where top differs from bottom

• 11 •

Conclusion

To conclude this 'should plastic be banned essay', it is safe to say that like any global problems affecting the environment and the people all over it is not easy to find a particular solution so we can only trust time to see what works and what doesn't and in the meantime find alternatives which are biodegradable and instead of dumping reuse and recycle and spread awareness about its importance, in this way you can contribute to maintaining nature's sanctity.